Verbs

© 2015 OnBoard Academics, Inc
Portsmouth, NH
800-596-3175
www.onboardacademics.com
ISBN: 978-1-63096-031-5

ALL RIGHTS RESERVED. This book contains material protected under International and Federal Copyright Laws and Treaties. Any unauthorized reprint or use of this material is prohibited. No part of this book may be reproduced or transmitted in any form or by any means, electronic or mechanical, including photocopying, reprinting, recording, or by any information storage and retrieval system without expressed written permission from the author / publisher.

OnBoard Academic's books are specifically designed to be used as printed workbooks or as on-screen instruction. Each page offers focused exercises and students quickly master topics with enough proficiency to move on to the next level.

OnBoard Academic's lessons are used in over 25,000 classrooms to rave reviews. Our lessons are aligned to the most recent governmental standards and are updated from time to time as standards change. Correlation documents are located on our website. Our lessons are created, edited and evaluated by educators to ensure top quality and real life success.

Interactive lessons for digital whiteboards, mobile devices, and PCs are available at www.onboardacademics.com. These interactive lessons make great additions to our books.

You can always reach us at customerservice@onboardacademics.com.

OnBoard Academics Workbook   K-2 ELA

Verbs

Key Vocabulary

verb

noun

action word

OnBoard Academics Workbook

K-2 ELA

Verbs
Verbs are action words.

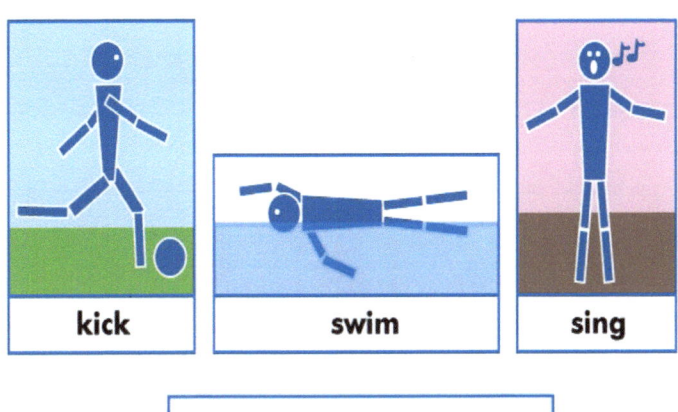

Sort the words.

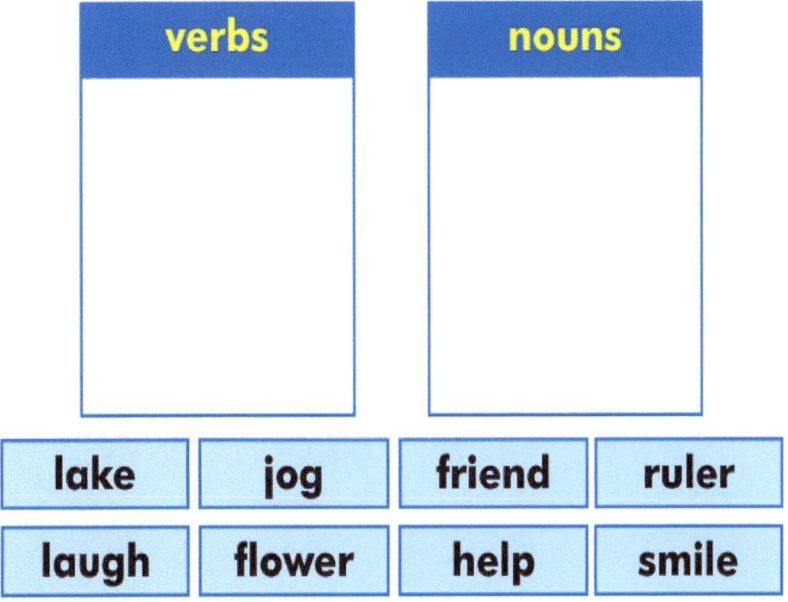

OnBoard Academics Workbook

K-2 ELA

Verbs at home and at school.
Fill in the boxes with verbs that describe things you do at home and things you do at school.

school	home

Highlight or circle the verbs.

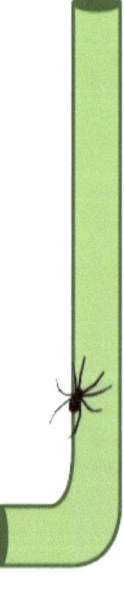

The itsy bitsy spider
Climbed up the water spout.
Down came the rain
And washed the spider out.
Out came the sun
And dried up all the rain,
And the itsy bitsy spider
Climbed up the spout again.

OnBoard Academics, Inc.   www.onboardacademics.com

OnBoard Academics Workbook K-2 ELA

Fill in the blanks with verbs.
Use the suggestions in the yellow boxes.

Mia _____ to music in the evenings. Her brother, James, likes to _____ TV. Both of them like to _____ on the computer and to _____. Mia _____ her music player last week. James _____ it behind the sofa.

| play | read | lost | looked |
| played | found | watch | listens |

OnBoard Academics Workbook

K-2 ELA

Add your own verbs.
Think of verbs for this text and fill in the blanks.

Mia likes to _bake_ cookies. James likes to _____ them! Last week, when she was _____ cookies, the telephone _____ . Mia was so busy _____ on the telephone that she _____ about the cookies, and they _____ . James didn't want to _____ any!

Name_____

Verbs Quiz

1. A verb is a person, place or thing. True or false?

2. Please _____ your hand if you want to speak.
   a. twist
   b. move
   c. wiggle
   d. raise

3. Mia _____ her cookies with James
   a. takes
   b. likes
   c. shares
   d. moves

4. Mom _____ her car.
   a. walked
   b. wished
   c. wrote
   d. washed

5. That joke made me _____.
   a. sleep
   b. cry
   c. laugh
   d. eat

OnBoard Academics Workbook   K-2 ELA

Verb Tenses

Key Vocabulary

verb

tense

past

present

future

OnBoard Academics Workbook — K-2 ELA

Verb Tenses
When does an action take place?

> The **tense** of a verb tells us when it takes place.

 Yesterday, James **cleaned** his room.

 Now, he is **riding** his bike.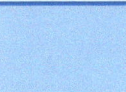

 Tomorrow, he **will read** a book.

Present   **Future**   **Past**

OnBoard Academics Workbook — K-2 ELA

Verb Tenses

Past	Present	Future
play**ed**	play**s**	**will** play
talk**ed**	talk**s**	**will** talk
work**ed**	work**s**	**will** work

Many past tense verbs end in **-ed**

Present tense verbs end in **-s** or do not change

Many future tense words use *will* plus the base verb

Complete the sentences with the correct verb tense.

Last week we...	Today we...	Next week we...
-ed	-s or no change	will + base word

will ride | hum | laughed | will spend
skate | juggled | will sing | help | hopped

OnBoard Academics Workbook — K-2 ELA

Check the box to label the verb tense.

	past	present	future
1. cleaned	☐	☐	☐
2. walks	☐	☐	☐
3. will wait	☐	☐	☐
4. calls	☐	☐	☐
5. practiced	☐	☐	☐

OnBoard Academics Workbook   K-2 ELA

Irregular Past Tense

Some past tense verbs *do not* end in *-ed*.

fly	give	have	sit
flew	gave	had	sat

Tic-tac-toe
Find three verbs in a row with irregular past tense.

pulled	lifted	ate
toasted	folded	wrote
shared	slipped	flew

Fill in the blanks.

Last week, the students _____ a mural.

The teacher _____ them cookies after they _____ all the paintbrushes.

Today, the class _____ poems.

Next week they _____ them out loud.

Name_____

Verb Tense Quiz

1. All verbs in the past tense end with the letters -ed. True or false?

2. What is the past tense of hug?
   a. hugs
   b. hugging
   c. hugged
   d. Squeezed

3. What is the future tense of smile?
   a. Smiled
   b. Will smile
   c. smiling
   d. smiles

4. Last year I _____ up the mountain.
   a. will hike
   b. hiked
   c. hiking
   d. hikes

5. I _____ my brother a train for his birthday.
   a. gived
   b. gibing
   c. gaved
   d. gave

Subject Verb Agreement

Key Vocabulary

subject

verb

helping verb

OnBoard Academics Workbook   Grade 3 ELA

> Some verbs do not show action; they show a **state of being**.

Underline the verb in each sentence.

The boy scored a goal.

He is excited.

OnBoard Academics Workbook — Grade 3 ELA

Using the verbs on at the bottom of the chart, complete the conjugation chart by filling in all of the boxes.

Pick a verb from each tense and write a sentence using that verb.

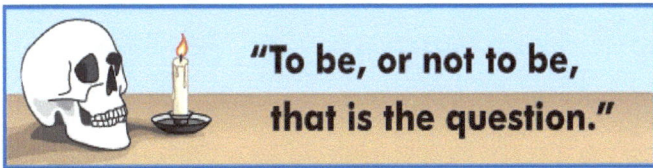

"To be, or not to be, that is the question."

present tense			past tense			future tense			
singular		plural	singular		plural		singular		plural
I		we	are	I	was	we	were	I	will be	we	
you	are	you		you		you		you		you	will be
he/she	is	they		he/she	was	they		he/she	will be	they	will be

am   is   are   was   were   will be

©2013 OnBoard Academics, Inc.   www.onboardacademics.com

OnBoard Academics Workbook Grade 3 ELA

Complete the sentences with the present tense of the verb to be.

We [ ] putting on a play.

Jenna [ ] the main character.

I [ ] making the costumes.

We [ ] very excited for the show.

Our families [ ] here to watch.

| am | is | are |

Fill in the blanks with the past tense of the verb to be.

> **The verbs was and were show the *past tense* of the verb to be and must agree in number with the subject of the sentence.**

I _____ sleepy this morning.

We _____ out late watching a movie.

There _____ green monsters in it.

It _____ very scary.

Grade 3 ELA

Find the missing verb and decide if it is singular or plural.
The first one is done for you as an example.

| am | is | are | was | were | S | P |

1. My class **is** studying dinosaurs. **S**
2. I ___ excited to learn about them. ___
3. Some species ___ as small as chickens. ___
4. The T-Rex ___ a meat eater. ___
5. The dinosaurs ___ extinct. ___

Helping Verbs

Helping verbs add detail to the way in which time is conveyed in a sentence. They are called helping verbs because they help other verbs show past tense, present tense or future tense.

Read the following sentences.
The sentences are organized by past, present and future. What is the difference between the first group and the second group?

_____

_____

Alison has cleaned her room.

Alison is cleaning her room.

Alison will clean her room.

The boys have helped her.

The boys are helping her.

The boys will help her.

OnBoard Academics Workbook — Grade 3 ELA

Circle the correct helping verb.

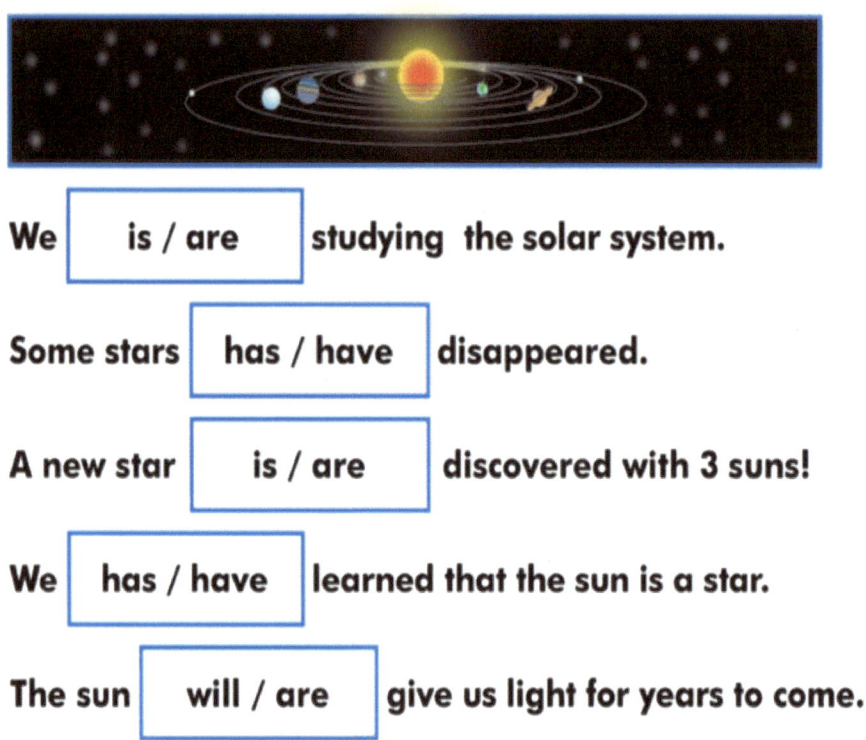

We [is / are] studying the solar system.

Some stars [has / have] disappeared.

A new star [is / are] discovered with 3 suns!

We [has / have] learned that the sun is a star.

The sun [will / are] give us light for years to come.

OnBoard Academics Workbook Grade 3 ELA

Subject Verb Agreement

> *Singular* subjects need *singular* verbs and *plural* subjects need *plural* verbs.

Put a check mark in the box next to the sentences that have subject verb agreement.

☐ Tory's teacher have finished handing out science reports.

☐ Tory was delighted with her science report.

☐ David will have a lot of explaining to do when he gets home.

☐ Owen's mom and dad is not happy with his report.

☐ The principal and vice principal was giving awards for the best reports.

☐ Jenna was given one of the awards.

Name_____

Subject Verb Agreement Quiz

1. The helping verb has is used with singular nouns. True or false?
2. Fred _____ washed the car. Circle the answer. was have has is.
3. We _____ going on a picnic. Circle the answer. are have has is
4. We _____ a new baby sister. Circle the answer. was have is were
5. The nurse _____ taking my temperature. Circle the answer. were have is has
6. The bicycle _____ a basket on the front. Circle the answer. has have is was
7. They _____ friendly kittens. Circle the answer. has were is was
8. My friends _____ all there too. Circle the answer. was have is were

www.ingramcontent.com/pod-product-compliance
Lightning Source LLC
LaVergne TN
LVHW010021070426
835507LV00001B/32